Poetic Gratitude

Poetic Graditude

Shift Your Mind Poetically

Harmeet Kaur Bharya

Matador
9 Priory Business Park,
Wistow Road, Kibworth Beauchamp,
Leicestershire. LE8 0RX
Tel: 0116 279 2299
Email: books@troubador.co.uk
Web: www.troubador.co.uk/matador
Twitter: @matadorbooks

ISBN 978 1838591 038

British Library Cataloguing in Publication Data.
A catalogue record for this book is available from the British Library.

Printed and bound in Great Britain by 4edge Limited
Typeset in 10.5pt Minion Pro by Troubador Publishing Ltd, Leicester, UK

Matador is an imprint of Troubador Publishing Ltd

CONTENTS

———∞∞∞———

About the Author   vi

Acknowledgements   viii

Introduction   1

Reflect and Educate   3

Contemplate and Influence   47

Accept and Inspire   94

About the Author

I was born and raised in the London Borough of Redbridge where I lived with my parents and sister. I started writing poetry at the age of sixteen and went on to study English Literature. I then studied Computer Science and started my career as a junior web developer at the University of Hertfordshire where I graduated.

Soon after, I married Mr Right, accepted a new job offer at Book Depository as a web developer, became pregnant and bought a house, all within nine months. After the birth of my daughter, I suffered with severe postnatal depression and anxiety for two years. After a year of maternity leave, I returned to work and became a project manager when Book Depository became a subsidiary of Amazon. Five years later I sadly miscarried an early twin pregnancy and decided to leave the Amazon family.

Thereafter, I suffered more heartache and debilitating anxiety; I was unable to leave home some days and was too scared to drive. My thoughts became morbid, and I started thinking of ways to end my life. However, with the help of professional and holistic therapies I made a steady recovery.

I am currently living in Berkshire with my amazing husband and beautiful daughter. It's now been three and a half years since I started working as accounts manager for my husband's business, Langhams Estate Agents.

The inspiration for my poetry stems from a timeline of sorrow and some very ugly experiences since the age of eleven to illness and the loss of loved ones, secondary infertility and miscarriage, and anxiety and depression. Whilst on the road to recovery, I discovered interior design and undertook further education in this field, exploring avenues to start a business. Unfortunately, I miscarried again after a further two years of trying for a second child.

In the midst of my spiritual healing, I revisited all the poetry I had been writing over the years, and began writing more each day. I haven't been able to put my pen down since this turning point, and published my first poetry book *Poetic Secrets* in 2018. I would best describe myself as a God-fearing soul, and my hobbies include yoga, meditation, interior design, poetry and playing the harmonium.

ACKNOWLEDGEMENTS

This book reflects my gratitude to God for giving me the experience of human life. I give thanks for sending me all those who have helped with my spiritual growth, and all the messages that made it possible to compile this collection of poetry. I am ever thankful to the Guru that lives within, who teaches me something new every day about myself and the world.

I am forever grateful to my father, Nirmal Singh Thethi, for being my greatest inspiration, my mother, Surinder Kaur Thethi, for being my pillar of support, my husband, Harminder Singh Bharya, for being my biggest motivation, my respected father-in-law, Gurdeep Singh Bharya, for his blessings, and my sister, Gurkiran Kaur, who has been my lifelong confidante. I thank my family and friends who have supported me through my journey, and send my heartiest compliments with gratitude to each person who has helped enable me to pen my poetry.

I dedicate this poetry collection to my daughter Harleen Kaur Bharya and children of the future, as this is a handbook that will offer important insights about life when most needed. Even if I am not there, I shall be present through these poetic messages.

INTRODUCTION

This is for you, completely and whole-heartedly for you. Take these poetic messages as fuel for your mind, comfort for your soul and balance for your body. Sieve out whatever it is you need at this point in your life. This is my way of sending out some truth with a positive angle, highlighting two sides of the coin and sharing some gratitude with you. These truths are not sugar coated; in some of these poems I speak directly to you, and in others I share my own experiences.

I want to shine light on the fact that life is a journey, and even after we have weathered some of our toughest fights, there are still parts of us we can keep working on. There is no end to personal development, and it's okay to have moments of feeling defeated and tired. Although we strive for positivity even in times of adversity, we are only human, and we needn't be hard on ourselves. I hope this poetry collection builds on some of what you already know, confirms what you are currently learning and brings you something new too.

I am currently exploring something I call 'life etiquette'. This is not about how we sit, stand or eat but more about how we treat people, speak and react to them, and the assumptions we make. My aim through poetry is to help us develop our own life etiquette, enabling us to carry ourselves consistently through life, emotionally, morally and spiritually, to create a more balanced life.

Only when I hit rock bottom did I find myself reflecting, and so I began to re-educate my mind. As I learnt more about myself and the world, I began contemplating my thoughts and actions, which influenced me to make changes within myself. As I began to see the world a little differently, I realised that that there is always more than one way to look at a situation.

It is so easy to make judgements based on the first thoughts that cross our mind, but that doesn't mean we are always right. In fact, often our clouded judgements cause the greatest misunderstandings in life and cost us what we value most. Often there is no wrong or right. Sometimes we are forced to accept that we won't always get the answers we want straightaway, maybe not even in our lifetime. Simply reducing my expectations has helped me to accept each situation for what it is, and it is this that has led me to share my insights in the hope of inspiring the world. I now believe this is my life purpose.

Writing wasn't a choice
the emotions just spilled
and words inked themselves
poetically ever flowing.

REFLECT AND EDUCATE

—⊶∞⊷—

Have you ever questioned your thinking patterns, your tendency to create scenarios and stories in your mind, and the outcome they may be having on your life?

I was trapped in a vicious circle of negative thoughts which I explored in my first book, *Poetic Secrets*. When I became aware of my thoughts I began reflecting on the impact they were having on me. My mindful cleansing exercises led me to channel the way I was thinking, and I began to rewire my thought processes. This taught me something very significant about the mind, body and soul connection.

"Conquer your mind and conquer the world"
– Guru Nanak Dev Ji

Rebirth

I write to feed your soul
with my gold dust,
helping you in your quest
to find your happy place.

I'm rebirthing my petals
with tender care.
Let's blossom together
and glisten like morning dew
diffusing aromas of jasmine
into our souls
as we take new breaths.

#feedyoursoul

LEARNING

—∞∞—

I don't conceal
the truth of my world;
if I did
how would you understand it.
I don't fear judgement;
if I did
how could I be the change
I want to see.
I don't follow the herd;
if I did
how could I be me.
I let you in
so I can learn from you
and you from me;
we can learn from each other
a better way to be.

#speakyourtruth

DETERMINATION

I am a poetess not a politician;
I know how to write my heart out,
but never learnt to converse
in tones of grey.
I listen twice as much as I speak
and know more than I ever show.
I don't entertain negativity;
in fact, it fuels my motivation,
heightening my need for expression,
provoking new thought,
boosting my energy and determination.
Nothing can ever break me;
my faith in the higher power
above and beyond
the strength of words
shall silence loud voices.

#seekmotivation

REFLECTION

Are you counting the moments
that made you happiest,
or multiplying the times
you've spent being sad?

Did your happiest mind
contend with your bravest heart
that it shifted your mind's eye
towards a sadness so effortless?

Did your saddest moments
make you lose sight
of the precious thoughts
that would warm your heart?

Was it easier being sad
when your happiness lost its way
in a place you no longer visited?

If you are still searching
for a way back to your happy place,
your longing will take you there.

#reflectoften

Imagine

Imagine breaking down
completely
right now,
feeling like you are living
your worst life
right now.

You blink an eyelid
and in front of you
stands another
making your worst life
look so fickle
right now.

#becomeaware

BREAK FREE

Vicious cycles cease
as soon as you refuse
to dance around with them.
The moment you become aware
of thoughts running rings around you,
the sooner you can begin
to reshape your life.

#breakthecycle

Contentment

———⊶⊷———

You have everything
yet you display all the signs
that you are incomplete;
perhaps it's time
to embrace with love
and celebrate with gratitude
all the blessings collecting dust.
There is always someone else
who would run a million miles
to take your place.
So wipe your slate clean;
great things are already there.

#countyourblessings

Bright Tomorrows

Yesterday was dark
today is a little lighter
tomorrow will be the brightest.

#seekthelight

MISCONCEPTIONS

Don't waste your time, energy and headspace
thinking of those who didn't show their face,
they stood there, empty handed,
their words failed to speak
their eyes fell asleep
their ears deafened.

You thought
they had lost all their senses
when time stood still for you.

But maybe
their hands were tied
when your fists were clenched,
their words were lost
when your silence spoke a thousand,
their tears were falling
but your lens was clouded,
they were all ears
but your ego could not hear.

When you thought
they didn't care,
maybe they were fighting a battle too.

Don't let assumptions
be the mother of misconceptions,
be unconditionally kind
to yourself and them,
gratitude coated in kindness
has a beautiful way of finding its way back to you.

#bemindful

UNITED

Let's dance the day away
Let's share the light today
Let's melt together in the sun
Let's mould our souls into one.

#stayconnected

WISDOM

Let's make each thought
a positive one.
Let's take our minds
to beautiful destinations.
Let's shape our future
with our magical wisdom.
Let's break away
from what holds us back.

#thinkpositively

THOUGHTS

You know those thoughts,
the ones that live caged,
the ones
that haven't been allowed to fly out,
those thoughts
are only as wide and wild as their residence,
let them come
and allow them to take wing swiftly,
think bigger
expand your mindset.

#spreadyourwings

JUDGEMENT

Sometimes it's easier to pretend
that you're doing okay
than to say that you are not,
it's easier to hide
behind a smile all day
when all you really want
is to drown in your frown all day.

It's more draining
trying to explain it all
than to keep quiet
and say nothing at all.

The struggle is real
the journey is rough
and rising is tough,
we can sit there and judge
with our absent care
but how can we be so sure
one day we won't be sitting in that chair.

#donthideaway

SMILE

Who doesn't want to wear
their most beautiful smile?
As life twists and turns
so does the crescent on one's face.

The domino effect falls
into lazy organs
moving placid fluids
through cracked canals
as sunken eyes cry blood
leaking into the valves
of a heart that drops
through a gloomy passage
into a gut that once absorbed
almost anything.

As mind collides with body
body with the soul
all cascades down
into fusions of shutdown
succumbing to a state so numb
that even tears leave you.

You awaken, you rise
you heal, you shine
through a smile
strong enough
to dry a million tears.

#keepsmiling

REMINDER

Negative thought patterns evolve
as sorrow becomes persistent
day after day
month after month
year after year,
multiplying into permanence
until sadness becomes your reality
and the misery of your insecurity
keeps you looking over your shoulder
waiting,
tempting fate
to knock you back down
just as you stand back up.
But that's the past;
you lived it
you survived it
you're stronger than ever
you're braver than ever
you're the happiest you've ever been;
let your past be only a reminder
not to let yesterday's cloud
dull today's sun.

#getbackup

SURVIVAL

I forced new breaths
grabbed new heartbeats
grafted new skin
tuned a new voice
carved new eyes.

When being strong
was the only choice,
I was born again,
it was agonising
but I survived.

#persevere

PAUSE SOMETIMES

I think and I feel
I run and I hide
I scream and I cry
from the mess in my mind.
Then
I pause and I heal
I breathe and I smile
I rest and I rise
until I cleanse my mind.

#keeprising

Transparent Soul

Like glass,
I break easily
and mend slowly.
Look through my transparent soul;
the cracks are state of the art.

#betransparent

HELP

⸺◦◦◦⸺

Let me hug your pain
so I can heal your wounds,
let me hold your hand
through your darkest days,
let me sweeten the bitter taste
in your mouth,
let me share the weight
of your heavy thoughts,
let me be the piece
that holds you together.

#buildyourtribe

MASTER

I've learnt how to measure
the inches of pain,
I can see right through
the skin that's frayed,
right into your seamless soul;
you can't fool a master
of her trade.
But I'm not here to judge
your loose ends,
I come with magic tailor made
to sew you right back up again.

#embracehelp

COMPASSION

You don't have to walk the same journey
to know how pain feels
tragedy strikes without warning
at no defined age
no place, no time, no pace.

There are too many scenes
to replicate a film
from a narrative only viewable in the mind,
the story is too long
and words are too weak
to describe such a twisted plot.

If you catch a glimpse of the preview
or someone whispers the highlights,
the moment you choose to
blind your sight
deafen your ears
and lose your tongue,
that's the moment
compassion becomes a choice.

#becompassionate

GENTLE

—⚬⚬⚬—

As deep hurt tears you apart
your mind loses contact with your heart.

The growing pain becomes violently sore
forcing your mind, body and soul to war.

But if you gently take a step back
desperate to get life back on track

You engage with the soul that lives within
which softly answers: 'where have you been'?

#connectyourmindbodysoul

DISTRACT YOURSELF

The sound of silence
awakens me
with a continuous ringing
in my mind,
reminding me
that I must do something
to channel this noise.

#beproactive

WORDS

———∞∞∞———

Words spoken
in a voice lighter
in a tone politer
can sound louder
than if you shouted.

#bepolite

Rebuild Yourself

Now that I wear a smile,
talk pretty words with a happy voice,
now that I look better, sound better, seem better,
suddenly I'm capable of anything.
But behind that fancy face
is someone who must double her effort
to keep pace with the rest of the world,
the day to day expectations,
the 'keep your life running' quota.
Imagine repairing your house everyday
with bricks and mortar;
this is what I must do everyday
to hold my broken pieces together.

#nevergiveup

WIN

Have you any idea
how many deep breaths
I must take some days
to keep going?

Do you realise
how many times I have to pause
to calm an internal storm
as its growing?

How often
I rescue myself
from what feels
like a near death experience?

Maybe next time
you'll be more mindful
when you see
a face so serious?

But I'm not alone
on this journey;
many of us
struggle.
Somedays
the fight is too tough
and so instead
we just crumble.

Even when we are better
after we have exhausted
all therapies under the sun,
we still have moments of defeat
even when we've won.

#keepwinning

STRENGTH

With your name, we take on challenges
that do not exist in your world,
we make sacrifices
to honour a commitment.

We endure blood, sweat and tears
to birth the fruit of your loins,
we bite our sore tongues
to keep our union sweet.

We smile to tame our loudest cries;
we are not unhappy, neither are we obliged.
These are the foundations laid for us,
this is all we have ever known:
to respect, to love,
to honour and sustain.

We are cultured but not weak;
we will always stand beside you
but never behind you.
Our struggle is what makes us strong.

#youarestrong

STABILITY

When you so carelessly share with me
the depths of your sadness, your broken pieces;
your sadness suddenly becomes mine,
worming its way into my flesh,
it begins gnawing into my soul
wreaking havoc in every part of me
that I had peacefully put to sleep.

So sometimes when you don't hear from me
for a few days or weeks
maybe I'm still shaking from the last time
catching my breath
drying my tears
cleansing my soul.

During my efforts to pick you up, I fell
and broke into a million pieces.
So don't be disheartened by my absence;
I'm thinking of you more than I should.
You can still lean on me, but I'm not the strongest.
Most importantly, I haven't forgotten,
I'm just replenishing my energy for next time.

#takecareofnumberone

TEARDROPS

If it's tears you need
to cry out all the residue
from a wounded heart,
cry a river
for you are healing.

#keephealing

INNER PEACE

In your neck of the woods
there's something
chipping away at you,
carving into your internal space
stealing your calm
as it chisels tiny fragments
from the blocks
you have been building
rebuilding, repairing
consistently, continuously.

When these days meet with you
hammer them down,
rise above its power
over you,
bash each nonsense strike
that comes at you
with the spade of hearts,
then dig deep to find self-love
and inner peace.

#findpeace

FLYING TO NEW LANDS

Leaving home is safe,
is the recent discovery
that pushed the priority
of crossing oceans
down to sea level.

I am still relearning
how to cross bridges
on the lands of a small island
and finding my feet,
sailing as far as the edges
of a coast that feels clear.
You need not ruffle my feathers,
for I am already in a zone
that feels out of my comfort.

I've spread my wings
as far as they can go,
and I'm already flying
reaching for new altitudes
as I grow ready.

#takesteadysteps

FREE YOURSELF

Nip it in the bud,
it's the only way to be free
and the most beautiful way to bloom.

#faceuptoit

GROWTH SPURT

One planted seed
prepares the soil
for more seeds:
a seed of ponder,
a seed of wonder
growing a weed of doubt.
Plant with positive deeds
and gaze as it spreads out.

#keepgrowing

WISDOM

You are not damaged goods,
your baggage is bursting with wisdom,
the path you've trudged
carried you to the top of your purpose.

You've won challenges
that don't get prizes,
you've walked to a hell
that's too deep to pen down.

But surely you can see the scars
of a journey that took you
to the most beautiful destination
where you found your happy place.

#bekindtoyourself

TOGETHER

—∞—

When
my mind
began to crumble

Your broken pieces
held me
together.

#talk

GRATITUDE

———⊗⊗⊗———

What made you so perfectly patient,
how did you know what I needed to hear
when words failed me.

How did you learn to be so gentle
when I was lashing myself,
what made you pause
to give me hugs in perfect timing.

When time wasn't ticking fast enough for me,
how did you learn to read my internal chaos
when I was silently still,
when did you learn to calm my storm
just before it destroyed me.

I'm touched by the way
you've put love into parts of me
I've been beating
and how you knew exactly
what to do
when I did not.

#begrateful

HAPPY PLACE

When I spoke, you listened
to understand, not to reply;
when I fell, you lifted me
from a dark hole
deeper than the ocean;
when I was bitter
you were sweet.
Your kindness did not fall
on deaf ears;
you were the light
to my darkness,
paving the way
to my happy place.

#findyourhappyplace

AFLOAT

—◦◦◦—

Your energy kept me going
when mine was running low,
I didn't even know
I was drowning
when you taught me
how to float.

#stayafloat

BEYOND FLAWS

I could see a beauty
behind the flaws of her skin
far beyond her flesh and bones
in a place sight could not reach,
in a space so raw and deep
that I travelled with my heart
to meet someone
I never knew.

#neverjudge

BEAUTY

—❧—

The dainty, frilly fuchsia
the bright and cheery sunflower
the flirtatious charm of rose
the golden hearted daisy
the elegance of the water lily
the stunning display of cherry tree.

They are much like us:
distinct names with diverse colours
dynamic shapes in different sizes
so delightful yet so delicate.
Next time you think of beautiful things
don't forget to count yourself in.

#youarebeautiful

HEAL

———⊶⊷———

These words write
to heal the scars
from every fall
that shaped every part of me,
how can I not share
the journey up to
the happy ever after.

#shareyourstory

Contemplate and Influence

—⚬⚬⚬—

I was able to shift my mindset and explore ways to turn negative situations into positive ones by simply thinking a little differently. By adopting the half glass full theory I was able to create better outcomes in my life. I found that consistency was key, and a sense of self-belief and confidence played a significant role. I learnt that even if I couldn't change a situation, I could certainly change my perception of it.

"You must be the change you wish to see in the world"
– Mahatma Gandhi

CONNECTION

―∞∞∞―

I understand
I really do,
I'm holding out the palm of my hand
to collect the teardrops
waiting to spill from your eyes.
You told your story
unintentionally displaying
some of your chapters
in the way you stood
the way you spoke
the way you stared
the way you smiled.
I noticed you
and your courage.
Our stories are different
but our pain is the same.

#shareyourpain

SELF-LOVE

———⊗⊗⊗———

I used to think
that pleasing everyone else
held the greatest importance,
that burning my energy
to warm the hearts
of others was superior,
and to be a pillar of support
was necessary.

When fulfilling the needs of others
became habit,
I stopped checking in on myself
and got so caught up
in creating happiness for others
that I forgot how to smile;
I began destroying my inner peace
and hardly paid myself any attention.

I lost the capacity to support me
because I had used all my fuel
trying to keep up
with the façade of my duties.
One day the penny dropped
I'd overlooked the most significant duty:
to take care of me, myself and I.
That day changed me forever.

I became the most important,
the warmth within my heart
became superior,
and I became supportive
of my own wants and needs.
I didn't become selfish, though
I learnt that I was no good to anyone
if I made a habit of leaving me
simmering on the back burner
where eventually I'd burn out.

#haveselfcompassion

Support

You dried my tears
with your warm heart;
I will never forget
how that made me feel.

#bekind

NEVER ALONE

I'm there with you
when your day becomes night
and your night becomes everlasting,
when the stars drift out of sight,
and the moon slides as it's passing
through black clouds, masking its light.
When this darkest solitude has you sinking,
losing yourself in a silent fight,
trapped in thoughts of ruinous thinking,
I'm there with you;
you are never alone.

#seekhelp

Mindfulness

———✦———

Let's lead with mindfulness,
let's use our senses
to see through different eyes
hear through different ears
think with a different mind
live in a different skin.
You'll see things
that will change your sight forever,
you'll hear things that will melt your heart
and open your mind to the unimaginable.
You'll find behind every person
a story untold.

#beunderstanding

THOUGHTS

My thoughts never cease
to amaze me;
they expose
how powerful they can be
in ways I never imagined
I'd live to see.

#staypositive

Moments of Glory

The mystery of the future
locks away our worries,
yet in the twisting and turning plot
of our life stories,
what makes us weep
shall help us leap
into our moments of glory.

#trusttheprocess

Admire

Don't you just admire
the way she steers her uncertainties
towards a path of open opportunities.

Don't you just admire
how she carries the weight of her worries
with a smile so contagious
that your mood begins changing status.

Don't you just admire
how her pretty soul
makes her face all the more beautiful,
the way she is so graceful
when her life is so painful.

Don't you just admire
the depth of her heart
the way she loves
the way she cares
the way she gives.

Don't you just admire
her optimism and her strength
her wisdom and her sixth sense.

Where would we be without her;
she is our wealth.
"From her kings are born".

#youarepowerful

Blossom

———∞———

I chose not to be a dot in the crowd,
I grew my petals with tender care,
I spend most days trying to blossom.
Be gentle with me;
sometimes I become bitter and I wilt,
some days I'm hanging by a thread.
I am delicate,
a flower with a heart;
watch me flourish
and plant more beautiful seeds.

#youareunique

SEEK

———∞———

Why be a fading dot in the crowd
When you can be so much more.
Cast your eyes on the grey
between the black and the white;
you'll find your shade right there.

#youarespecial

LIFE

———∞∞∞———

You've only just arrived,
don't leave a life unlived,
you've only touched the surface
don't abandon your purpose,
you must live
because heaven can wait.

#seekpurpose

Remember

There is beauty in everyone;
perhaps those with bitter minds
are the ones with broken hearts.
Let's not forget
the journey we travelled
to be where we are.

#useyourwisdom

DIFFERENCES

In someone's time of need
if you are able to place
your differences to one side
and be with them
at least in your thoughts
you are already half way
towards conquering your ego.

#workonyourego

DISTANCE

———⚉———

Let's close the distance
between our worlds,
let's tear the pages
that separate us,
let's fine-tune the chords
to keep us dancing in rhythm,
let's stay connected
and not lose sight of each other.

#reachout

TRY

I can't, I can
I will, I won't
be the one
to hold me back.

#youcan

MIND CHALLENGE

———❦———

Challenge your thoughts
not your strength,
for you are only
as strong
as your beliefs.

#believeinyourself

INNOCENCE

———∞∞∞———

Use the wisdom of today
to take you to the next,
linger close to your innocence
as if you were born just yesterday.

#staygrounded

ACKNOWLEDGE

Acknowledge the wounds
that became scars,
they will reciprocate
in ways
you cannot imagine.

#scarsareyourstrength

CREATE CHANGE

We seek change
in places where the sun hasn't risen,
we envisage
a picture perfect world,
mindless to abstract existence.
Let's not force change
onto others,
but create change within ourselves
which is beyond beautiful,
that multiplies
to infinite channels
so graciously.

#createchange

LESS IS MORE

———❧———

We glance across
the greenest grass
discovering rich souls bathing
in a pool of happiness.
As deceit fiddles
with the deluded mind
our eyes drift over
to the richest poor
revealing less is more.

#findcontentment

VOICE

––––⌘––––

Sometimes silence speaks louder
than a scream,
desperate to burst
through sealed lips,
what is left unsaid
is seen in the mirrors
of your face.

#speakup

SAFE

Whatever it is you dread,
the fears that lead your tears,
whatever thoughts you think
that torture your delicate mind,
whatever body you live in
no matter how crippling the pain,
know
that your soul will always
be safe.

#youaresafe

Lotus Flower

———

Once you conceive the idea
of detaching your mind
from your body of dust
and tune
into your timeless soul,
the pain you endure
emotionally or physically
becomes more bearable
and any consequences
begin to perish,
reshaping your perception
of the mind-body-soul connection.

#takebackcontrol

PURPOSE

—∞∞—

Stay close to your purpose:
remember why you started,
harness the reasons,
channel the choices,
create the wildest vision,
reach the greatest of goals
with the strongest strategy.

#makeithappen

Uncertainty

—∞—

In our moments of uncertainty
we position our mind outwards
for insightful guidance
to determine life-changing answers
from the pool of possibilities.

Everyone needs a friend
to share this rise and fall,
though you will find
your greatest friend is
the Guru within.

#meditate

BRIDGES

Don't burn bridges
that endured you
when you were on fire.
Shower with love
the souls
that are burning.

#helpothers

Shift Anger

———◦◦◦———

Talk yourself out of anger
and save your soul
from burning in fiery flames,
by watering down
the wild fires
that fuel your mind.

#dontstayangry

Awareness

———∞∞∞———

When we learn to listen
twice as much as we speak
we are able to absorb ourselves
into deeper thought
and observe the silence
spilling thousands of tears
the loudest cry could never speak.

#alwayslistenfirst

SUPPRESSION

———∞∞———

We suppress what consumes us
with all our strength,
fight useless thoughts
with all our might.

But we are no God,
so at times
our human flesh crumbles
as do our towering minds.

We have moments
of weakness
but each time we rise
we stand a little taller.

#youarehuman

PAIN

———∞∞∞———

When we ourselves
endure pain
only then
can we understand
another's hurt.

#becaring

SKIN

It was not what you said
nor what you showed,
but what you did
that moulded
every curve and edge
to shape a sense of secureness
in a skin that feels kind to my soul.

#speakkindly

SILENT KINDNESS

It matters most
what you do
when no one is watching;
kindness in silence
is worth more
than praise,
bringing the kind of bliss
that feeds your soul.

#stayhumble

RAINBOWS

If ever you meet eyes
with someone wearing a frown,
whisper the kind of melody
which is not only music to their ears
but comfort to their heart.
Make upside down smiles
a priority like no other,
with your sunshine and their rain,
paint the rainbow they need to see.

#helpeachother

VALUE

———⚒———

Let's bury the thought
of taking our hats off
to those as they are placed
in their graves;
let's help them rise
whilst they are amongst us.

#valuelife

SPEAKING OUT

The fear of bare bones
visible to a world of judges
feeds the insecurities within,
restraining us from speaking out.
We can hide from the world
but not from our truth,
our souls are always naked
and the creator misses nothing.

#betruthful

BLESSINGS

—∞—

Waving your blessings
in the face of broken dreamers
is never going to warm them
but rather salt their wounds.
Your actions will dishearten them
more so than your blessings.
Help them find a happy place
in your joyous moments
by recognising their sorrow
and surely they will celebrate with you.

#thinktwice

DEFINITION

—∞∞∞—

Black and white shades
will never define you
nor the picture the world paints of you.
The images you carry of yourself
hold a value which resembles
the best version of you.

#staytruetoyourself

SUITCASE OF MEMORIES

It's time to let go;
pack it up,
lock it tight,
throw away the key.

I remembered more
as I tried to forget
the suitcase of memories
that were taking me
on a life-changing journey,
unpacking the hurt
that would heal me.

#acknowledgethehurt

Express Yourself

———

Dig deep for your creativity,
sketch maps
with your aesthetic riches
that can guide us
to make sense of the world.
Explore the complexities of life,
open up those difficult emotions
in times of uncertainty.

You have an art
perhaps undiscovered,
an outlet
to express yourself.
Through expression
we can educate each other,
influence the positive change
screaming for attention.

Together
we can inspire the world
with our wisdom
and be a comfort
with our kindness.
When we are united
we are suddenly capable
of so much more.

#seekinspiration

FEED YOUR SOUL

The best version of you
can only prosper
as much as you hydrate
the thirsty soul
with wholesome moments.

#keephydrated

LET IT GO

—⸰⸰⸰—

Imagine your mind
as the sky
and your thoughts
as fluffy clouds
passing by.

#freeyourmind

SPEAK

Sometimes there is so much to say
that we can't speak.
Don't allow sealed lips
to lock you on the inside;
find a way
to express yourself.

#findavoice

MIDDLE GROUND

There are grounds
between passive
and aggressive,
that abide by tough
without the rough,
emerging smooth
with the truth,
intuitively balancing
the undefined boundaries,
by bouncing the sound
of what proves assertive.

#beassertive

BREAK FREE

Crush the demons
holding you back,
thrust away the pain
that corners your mind,
seek the power
that enlightens your soul
releasing an energy
pure and whole,
calming the noise
and cleansing the path
for seasons of joy
that fill your void.

#fillthevoid

SURPRISES

Blessings break their silence
arising at unexpected times,
catching you by surprise,
lifting the soles of your feet
from the grounds you kneeled upon
and cried.
You'll be swept up and lifted
when your hour arrives,
you shall be honoured
to know someone is always
listening in awe and being inspired.

#giveunconditionally

ACCEPT AND INSPIRE

I've learnt that there are certain things in this world I cannot change, whether people or circumstances. I've struggled with this my whole life until now. But by changing myself and my thoughts I have been able to accept many things that are out of my control. Instead I've put energy into the things I can influence, and found purpose through this journey of seeking change. If I accept things as they are, I can have a happier and more fulfilling life. I have found a way to see the good in each situation, even when it's a struggle, and I hope to inspire others to do the same.

"I alone cannot change the world, but I can cast a stone across the waters to create many ripples"
– Mother Theresa

CHANGE

Let's educate minds
with the vision to influence change
that will inspire the world.

#bethechange

REALITY

Sometimes we coat hidden realities
with kind words
to sustain our inner peace.
We are no different
if we spite the pain
that helped us rise.
We cannot please the world,
yet we conceal our loudest cries.
We remain authentic
by staying true to ourselves;
reality will reveal itself
by shining through the
windows of kind souls.

#remainauthentic

COMFORT

Be all ears;
it's the best comfort
for those heartbeats
that are fluttering.

#helpsomeone

Loving Yourself

There's a part of me
always feeling scrunched up
as if it's forgotten
how to be unfolded,
free from creases.
So I've accepted
and learnt to love
that part of me
I can't quite iron out.

#acceptyourflaws

LOVE

If the sun ceases
to smile within,
seek warmth
from what you love,
and what you need
shall come.

#dowhatyoulove

Timing

‐‑⊗⊗⊗‑‐

The here and now is easier
than the reckoning of tomorrow,
blissful ignorance is a blessing
enabling our presence in the present;
let the future reveal itself
in its own perfect timing.

#focusonnow

SPOKEN

As we crossed paths
our silence spoke
in a momentary gaze
only our souls understood.

#connect

Thank You

— ◈ —

Thank you for opening your arms
on my return from hiding away;
thank you for fuelling my poetic charm
when my words had stalled for days
in my moments of absence;
thank you for keeping a candle burning for me
when I was sitting in absolute silence.

#givethanks

Metamorphosis

Some days I'm not strong enough
to face the world,
so I remain in my cocoon.
Some days I'm the caterpillar
and on others I'm the butterfly.
Every day is a new birth.

#startagain

DIFFERENT

———◦◦◦———

I'm not like you;
I must live in the confines of my safety net,
I've journeyed all the therapies under the sun
so I can at least survive.

I'm not like you;
I'm restricted by the panic
that makes my legs tremble on motorways,
my heart skip beats in an aeroplane,
my mind quiver at the thought of a new pill.

I'm not like you;
I'm too complicated to understand,
I don't come with instructions,
I can't operate like a robot.
I need breaks,
sometimes long ones,
and sometimes I drain
my own batteries.

I'm not like you;
I need at least eight hours sleep
or I'm dizzy and disorientated,
dragging my heels all day,
fighting closing eyelids.

I'm not like you;
a day inside me
and you'd flee,
you'd see how hard I work
all day, every day, to keep functioning.

I'm not like you;
but I know my smile
is worth a million,
and that's enough
to take me to the next day.

I'm not like you;
but neither are you like me.
We are all different
on our journey
writing our unique story.

#beyourownkindofbeautiful

BLISS

———◆———

One day a gleam of enlightenment
shall emerge.
I'll begin drifting
into a realm of radiant light,
discovering my soul
floating in ivory pearls,
in tranquillity, soaking in a mist
of beautiful energies,
detached like the lotus flower,
absorbed in bliss.

#daretodream

TIME

This time-boxed life of mine
gives me measured moments to shine.

Awakening a light that shines the brightest,
merging with a power that stands the highest.

This fickle life will be over so soon,
above and beyond the stars and moon.

These treasures of mine shall not follow me,
this is the truth of reality.

I shall not fritter this time away
instead I will reflect, connect and pray.

A mindful energy suspends any confusion,
life is the most beautiful form of illusion.

#makeeachdaycount

POWER

—∞∞—

What will be
will be
if it's meant to be.

Give your worries
to the higher power
and watch the magic unfold.

#everythingwillbefine

GIFT

Our darkest endings
reveal our brightest beginnings;
as we lose our hopeless fear
we find our long-lost purpose,
and our greatest despair
brings us our greatest gift.

#dreambig

GRACEFUL

―⁂―

Our challenges are only as tough
as we see them;
our upward struggles are as high
as we take them.
Hustle through the noise;
climb each step gracefully.

#begraceful

CLARITY

Dust away the pile of thoughts
settled in the midst of a chaotic mind,
gently wipe away the mess
sitting like tiny crumbs of fuss.

Shift the infuriated mind's eye,
clarity will soon be there.
As filthy options are disposed of
cloudy judgements shall disappear.

#practicemindfulness

STEADY

If the bare minimum is all you can manage,
do as little as you need today;
your world will not collapse
into nothingness
but if nothing changes,
you may.
Be the hands of your clock,
tick as slow or as fast as is comfortable.

#takeyourtime

Flawless

She is not flawless
neither are her choices,
though her reasons are faultless.
Her imperfections are shaping her
broken curves and edges.
Even when she is so far
from the path we want her to see,
we love her
just the way she is.
Let's not try to change her
but change ourselves;
for we too are not flawless.

#donotcompare

FORGIVENESS

It takes a skilled mind
to erase memories of a trodden heart;
to forget you must remember,
and remembering carves the cracks,
reminding forgotten hurt how to ooze.
When forgetting is near impossible,
make forgiveness possible.

#forgive

Tomorrow

I've witnessed the length of time
granted to souls with the shortest lives,
the ones that lived on borrowed time,
fighting for the moments that never arrived,
stealing moments in a life so bittersweet,
shaping a smile that feels complete.
Let's waste no golden breath
nor skip a wondrous heartbeat,
for tomorrow is never promised.

#liveyourlife

LOST ONES

I miss them dearly,
the ones who have passed
into realms of unknown worlds
far and beyond the reach
of my empty hands;
instead of burying
my head into sadness
I rub an ounce
of their wisdom into myself
to keep them alive.

#learnandgrow

Harmony

I pour into myself
the absent love
I would seek
from people in places
that couldn't love me.

I embrace the delight
as the world concurs
with the connection to oneself.

I've learnt how
to keep pouring
drops of love
into the river of my soul
and find myself flooded
in blissful harmony.

#loveyourself

MAJESTIC

———∞———

We dissolve
our patterns of the past
as we poise our present
on the lessons we learnt
all the times we fell
into a self-inflicted mess.
We cannot change in haste,
but evolve majestically;
it is not wasted
what taught us
how to free ourselves
from future pains.

#freeyourself

Endurance

To endure the pain
of what is beyond control
I create new pathways
that take me farther
in moments of weakness,
glazing my inhibitions
with a scented sweetness,
seeking a happier place
filled with contentment.

#thinkhappythoughts

Yesterdays

As cold, clingy, compulsive scenes
circulate in the muddled mind
of a true story so unkind,
even persuasive words
would fail to replicate
every coarse memory
that ruffled the calm,
each time eyes close
curtains open,
action replays
and coping crumbles,
composure is crushed
as floodgates open
to a million more disturbing yesterdays
that refuse to leave.
You cope, you compose
you rise as you fall,
blooming like a rose.

#youareafighter

AFFIRM

I shall shield my heart
against the harm of a stormy pain
I shall not wither
but stand stalwart,
as I dare let shift
the eye of my mind.

I shall not drift
nor run away
in the hurricane lift
but remain in steady bliss,
merging with tranquil winds
as negativity is dismissed.

#findsolace

BLESSING

When you least expect it,
when you need it most
the thoughtfulness you sprinkled
will shower you seamlessly.
Kindness is never forgotten;
the rewards are timeless,
arriving as priceless blessings
in disguise.

#bepatient

SOUL CONNECTION

We cross paths;
smiles across the wall each day
with quick hellos
in our shortest minutes,
the deepest convos
and the longest walks.

If blood is thicker than water,
then why does the thinnest water
feel more like beautiful blood,
and why does a connection
feel stronger than it should.

The heart has no bounds;
it connects with what feels
like its own kind,
when you're touched
in your weakest moments
the heart births a special place.

#createfriendship

LOVE

Love can break through
the coldest ice heart,
love can tame the flames
burning in a fiery mind,
love can conquer
the toughest fight,
love can fill kindness
into parts of a broken heart;
when you choose love
you can never hate.

#chooselove

124

OPPORTUNITY

———

Opportunity is found
in second chances
to live the dream
that shattered
many moons ago.
Memories
that feel sore
can be dispelled,
imagine them
as tiny particles decaying
as you renew your stay.

#givesecondchances

CYCLES

We put it on ourselves,
restricting new beginnings
we could have started yesterday,
placing a tangled pressure
on our own minds to succeed,
conforming to the constraints
of man-made timing.

A new beginning
a new idea
a new mind set
can begin on any new day;
new thought
is all you need
to release you from spinning
in cycles of new years.

Challenge your mind
to the power of now;
it can take you anywhere
you want to be.

#shiftyourmindset

TRUE COLOURS

Choose openness
to set you free,
talk out your thoughts
to clear out your mind,
let yourself cry
to release the heaviness,
be transparent
to make you feel real;
your internal space
will thank you
for displaying
your true colours.

#beopen

HALF GLASS FULL

I've spent too much time
in this short life of mine
pouring energy
outwards,
filling half-full glasses
for anyone but me.

When my glass
became half empty
it was my most important lesson
and greatest learning.

That feeling
is imprinted within
as a permanent reminder
to replenish my own glass
with love, respect
and compassion inwards.

These new rules of living
shall keep me
from falling into old traps
that no longer serve me.

#fillyourglass

FREEDOM

———✸———

I floated through depression
as if drifting
in and out of consciousness.

By keeping my head above water
I broke out of a sinking trance
and freedom suddenly swept in.

#keepgoing

Fun Times

———

There are days
when I feel
like a child
trapped inside a mind
too ripe to play and giggle.

My curiosity cradles
the child in me
affirming that I am allowed
to be as young or as old
as I feel.

#keephavingfun

DIFFERENT VIEWS

There is quite a fine line
between influencing
what is important
to the core of our being,
and pushing spoonfuls into innocent minds.

We can share our wealth of wisdom
so long as we are aware
that their choice is theirs,
just as we have ours.

We cannot possibly think the same
nor will our wants and needs always align.
We birthed our perspectives worlds apart,
so we must respect
that each is unique and just as valid.

It is our fears that steer us
to fight passionately for our beliefs,
but let us not forget
who gave us this gift.

When we cannot change
what is out of our tired hands,
let us calm the storm in our wild mind
and accept the will of the higher power
that all shall resolve and unfold just as it should.

#worrylesspraymore

EQUALITY

Give her the kind of beginning
that will empower her mind
and toughen her soul
to fight for fairness;
inspire her
to rise and roar
as she claims her place
beside the lions
laid on the throne;
as flesh parts womb,
gift change
to these new beauties,
welcome her with open arms,
honour her god-gifted breath.
Her worth is beyond praise.

#befair

LEAD CHANGE

Let's raise boys
to be the kind of men
that could not just cope
if all women vanished,
but extend their hearts
beyond bread and butter.
If we begin closing the gap
for girls yet to be born,
we may live to see the change
we only yearned for.

#leadbyexample

LAW OF ATTRACTION

———∞∞∞———

Send out the kind of energy
that is fragrant
and so flattering
that it returns to you
scented with the gratifying
pleasures you attracted.

#sendoutpositivity

TRANSPARENT

———

We open the curtains,
inviting the whole world
into parts of us
that were wounded,
tender and vulnerable,
broken and constantly healing,
in the hope
of giving a wider lens
deeper insights
different perspectives;
hoping maybe
just maybe
to channel mind sets
and plant seeds
that channel thoughts,
paint pictures
to see a little clearer,
to pour an ounce of consideration
into oblivious minds,
to place a sliver of compassion
into unconscious hearts.
Acceptance overrules
that not everyone changes,
for all hearts beat a little differently.

#accept

PERSEVERANCE

It wasn't easy
revisiting those tender moments
that had me weeping
for what felt like a lifetime.
I looked backwards,
rewinding the film,
dreading the replay of hurt
for the sake of inspiring
even one soul
amongst the thousands
that suffer in silence.
Disappointments won't keep me
from trying again,
for I will keep going
until I pull away
the wool that covers
a million eyes.

#inspire

SELF CONFIDENCE

———⊷⊶———

You are
what you feel you are,
not what they say you are.

You are
the beauty inside of you,
not what they see outside of you.

You are
what you want to be,
not what they expect you to be.

You are
more beautiful
than you think you are.

You are
in control of shaping
who you are.

#youareathingofbeauty

Surrender

Only when
you surrender yourself
can you begin
releasing fears
from the teacup
that is brewing
a storm
that isn't really there.

#faceyourfears

Acceptance

———— ✦ ————

Life is as we choose to view it.
The view is wider
when we look
through the lens of acceptance.

#keepanopenmind

LESSONS

———❧———

If today were to be my last
these would be my lessons from the past:
Fight the battles that I lost,
rise from the falls that made me soft,
find a voice that speaks a thousand words,
stay true to yourself and avoid the herds,
never shy away from truth,
lead with compassion; learn to soothe,
stand highest in your lowest of times
remember that every story has two sides,
if ever you find yourself feeling alone
look within to find your rising rainbow,
keep on with the dreaming and achieving
if ever you fail never give up on believing,
let kindness lead the way
don't let ego steal your radiant ray,
if ever you feel as delicate as glass
ground yourself by walking on grass,
aspire to be as strong as steel
strength will come as you pray and kneel,
coat yourself in a beautiful mist
treat all that you have as a gift.

#makeityourbestlife

Stay Blessed

I have shared with you poetically some of my deepest thoughts, toughest lessons and most valuable insights that help me to cope with what I cannot change. I hope there has been something new for you that has perhaps helped you to contemplate and reflect, and had a positive influence on your mind. Most of all, I hope that you have learnt something about acceptance and gratitude, and that it has inspired you to think a little differently or confirmed that there is someone else who thinks just like you.

This need not be the end; if you are inspired and wish to read more, connect with me on Instagram: harmeetkaurbharya.

 Matador